St. Julian

An Opera

Richard A. Hawley

with drawings by M. W. Hawley

Bits Press
Cleveland

Copyright © 1987 by Richard A. Hawley

Bits Press
Department of English
Case Western Reserve University
Cleveland, Ohio 44106

ISBN 0-933248-08-3

For Martin and Joyce

If music be the food of love, play on . . .

HAGIOGRAPHICAL NOTE

The historical record contains no definitive—nor even any reliably factual—account of St. Julian the Hospitaller. There are only stories. The earliest are set in the 4th century in Egypt; subsequent tellings proliferated through the 13th century and place Julian elsewhere along the Mediterranean and in Europe. In some of the tales he fights valiantly in the Crusades. What is common to all accounts and no doubt the basis of his sainthood is that Julian lived the closing years of his life in voluntary chastity and asceticism. He (and in some accounts his wife, Basilissa) gave lodging and comfort to travelers and the poor; thus his title "hospitaller."

In the closing years of the 13th century, James of Voragine composed an authoritative Lives of the Saints, the English title of which became *The Golden Legend*. It is the *Golden Legend* account, a romance, which is best known and best loved. In this version, Julian is a nobleman skilled at arms who unintentionally kills his mother and father. In reparation he undertakes a severe penance of self-denial and service. When he gives succor to a dying and particularly repulsive old man, he is reestablished in God's grace and is raised at once to heaven.

In Rouen Cathedral St. Julian's story is pictured in stained glass. Gustave Flaubert noted it with fascination as a boy and referred to it in several works over the course of his writing life. Although he would study many medieval texts carefully before composing his arresting story, "The Legend of St. Julian the Hospitaller" (1876), the window in Rouen and a dream he had as a young man were the two principal inspirations for his St. Julian. In the dream Flaubert and his mother are walking deep in a forest filled with monkeys. As the monkeys press in on him, Flaubert shoots one of them in the shoulder and it shrieks in pain. Flaubert's mother reproaches him, "Why do you wound your friend? . . . Don't you see that he loves you?"

In Flaubert's tale, Julian's impulses to kill what he loves and to love what he kills are reconciled as part of a divine plan for his life. The reconciliation of these dreadful urges is also the subject of this opera.

R.A.H.

ST. JULIAN

ACT I/THE CURSE

A wise and prosperous Lord and his Lady preside over the ordered splendor of the castle, court, and lands of an estate in medieval France. In the course of a festival celebrating the birth of their long-awaited son, Julian, both mother and father are visited, separately, by a strange hermit-gypsy who tells each a cryptic prophecy. To Julian's mother: "Thy son shall be a saint"; to his father: "great bloodshed, great glory."

Julian's father and mother are well-pleased as the boy grows in health and piety. Moved, as a boy is moved, to pursue and to kill animals, Julian finds himself powerfully aroused at killing a mouse in the estate chapel and a pigeon on the castle ramparts. When it is determined that he is ready to learn the Hunt, Julian enters into the deadly art with a grace and facility that replace everything else in his understanding. He becomes a poet of the deft kill, an athlete of animal slaughter. At the culmination of a long, unworldly night of ecstatic slaughter, Julian slays an uncountable number of stags trapped in a defile. The last, just before expiring, addresses Julian in speech: "Accursed! Accursed! Accursed! Some day, ferocious soul, thou wilt murder thy father and thy mother!"

Sickened for months by this prophecy, Julian resolves never to hunt or to bear weapons again. When he recovers, however, he is persuaded to resume his nobleman's training in arms, at which he once again proves himself adept. One summer evening, on the castle grounds, when a flutter of white catches his eye, he impulsively hurls his javelin at the imagined stork. A piercing cry is heard as the javelin passes through the long white stream of his mother's cap and nails it to the wall. In abject dread, Julian leaves the castle forever.

ACT II/THE CRIME

Julian becomes an adventurer-crusader. Giving full vent to his lethal energy and skill, he fights valiantly and victoriously in all regions, in all climes, throughout the known world. He shields orphans, widows, and the aged from harm. He aids nobles in peril, republics besieged. When Julian and his troops rescue the Emperor of Occitania from imprisonment by Moorish infidels, Julian is given the Emperor's daughter in marriage and a princely living in return.

One night Julian's domestic calm is broken by a renewed urge to hunt, and he takes to the surrounding woodlands with his bow and quiver. That same night, a threadbare but dignified pair of pilgrims, an aged man and a woman, seek hospitality at Julian's castle. To his wife's astonishment and delight they are revealed as Julian's father and mother, who have taken up the pilgrim's life in quest of their lost son. Julian's wife gives the elderly couple gracious hospitality, including Julian's and her own bedchamber.

Meanwhile, in the course of his night's hunt, Julian finds he is unable to deal a death blow to any of the hundreds of animals he encounters. Birds, serpents, predators and prey of all descriptions close about him and accompany him back to the castle.

Entering his bedchamber in the dark, he detects a bearded man lying beside what he assumes to be his wife. With unreflecting passion he draws his dagger and brutally dispatches the sleeping couple.

Aware of the depth and completeness of his crime, he arranges the funeral of his parents, forsakes all possessions, and, wearing only a monk's robe, takes to the roads to beg.

ACT III/THE REPARATION

Wherever Julian goes, he tells his story: of his curse and of its fulfillment. He is reviled and shunned by all.

Making his way to a river crossing in a desolate, inhospitable waste, Julian resolves to devote the rest of his life to ferrying travelers across the often-swollen river. For his labors he asks nothing in return.

One bitterly cold and stormy night, Julian is called out of his sleep by a traveler at the far side of the crossing. The voice addresses him by name. Making his way across the river, Julian finds his caller unutterably repulsive: emaciated, leprous, reeking. The stream rages and the passage back is perilous. Once ashore and sheltered in Julian's hovel, the leper demands food, then drink, then rest. Julian offers the leper his own bed, and, when the leper complains repeatedly of cold, Julian offers the warmth of his own naked body.

Thus embraced, Julian ascends up and out of the hovel, face to face with the Risen Christ.

ST. JULIAN

# THE CURSE

(*A feast is in progress: joyous dining, drinking, and revelry. A son has been born to the Lord and Lady of the Manor. Julian's father presides over the celebration. Julian's mother lies alone in a remote chamber of the castle. Her bed chamber is barely visible in silver-blue light. Festive noise gives way to the raising of a toast.*)

Chorus: To thy blood! To Julian!
(bass voice)   Long may he live in Christ!

(trio):   New life to thee, sire,
Our lord hath granted
Bounty from every true seed
Thou hath planted.

(all):   A son, a seed; a seed, a son;
Blessings, sire, from the blessed One.
Son of thy seed, seed of the Son,
Blessings, sire, from the blessed One.

(trio):   A son is a story,
Each story is true,
In God's great foreknowing
Each story is new.

(all):   A son, a seed; a seed, a son;
Blessings, sire, from the blessed One.
Son of thy seed, seed of the Son,
Blessings, sire, from the blessed One.

(trio):   A son is a promise
To bear thy blood,
The day's bright dawning,
The rose's bud.

(all):   A son, a seed; a seed, a son;
          Blessings, sire, from the blessed One.
          Son of thy seed, seed of the Son,
          Blessings, sire, from the blessed One.

(trio):   A son is a hero,
          The son and his sword
          Will bloody creation
          For our dear Lord.

(all):   A son, a seed; a seed, a son;
          Blessings, sire, from the blessed One.
          Son of thy seed, seed of the Son,
          Blessings, sire, from the blessed One.

(trio):   A son is a sorrow,
          A sire must weep.
          A son takes the path
          That a son must keep.

(all):   A son, a seed; a seed, a son;
          Blessings, sire, from the blessed One.
          Son of thy seed, seed of the Son,
          Blessings, sire, from the blessed One.

          (*Moonlight over* mother*'s bed chamber. A shadowy
          cloaked figure, the* hermit, *makes his way toward the
          chamber.* Mother *sits, takes up her baby from his crib.*)

Mother: What? There—who is there?
          My lord, is it thee?

          Speak, pray. Say thy will.
          Is it a man I see?

Hermit: Fear not, my lady, and rejoice.
          God bless thee and thy son.

Indeed, thy son shall be a saint.
A saint thy son shall be!
And when his final battle's won,
And when his holy grief is done,
He'll rise a saint, thy Julian,
By Christ, a saint he'll be.

Mother: Sir, wait! Kindly rest.
Say more, dark shade, of this.

Hermit: (*Receding into darkness*)
And when his holy grief is done,
He'll rise a saint, thy Julian . . .

Mother: Gone—and left us darkly blessed,
I feel more dread than bliss.
Has joy or grief disturbed our rest?

(*The banquet is dispersing. As the guests depart, singing, Julian's* father *follows them down the steps into the night.*)

Chorus: A son, a seed; a seed, a son;
Blessings, sire, from the blessed One.
Son of thy seed, seed of the Son,
Blessings, sire, from the blessed One.

(*An ear-ringed* gypsy *emerges*)

Father: Thou! There in the mist!
Come forward and present thyself.
May I hear thy business?

Gypsy: This, sire, only this:
The joy thou celebrates tonight
Is greater, greater than thou knows.

Thy Julian is for glory, sire,
Thy bounty overflows.
Glory, empire, blood in rivers,
His flashing blade, his deathly blows—

Father: Enough! What's this? Come back, I say!
Back among the mists he goes.
This dark man's raving stirs me deep.
It troubleth a father's sleep.

(*Festal light darkens to moonlight.*)

Father's, :   This dark man's   . . . Greater, greater
  Gypsy's   Raving stirs me deep.   Than thou knows,
   voices   It troubleth   Thy bounty
               A father's sleep.   Overflows.

(*Daylight in the palace courtyard. All is bright, orderly, and opulent.*)

Chorus: This is the bountiful, peaceable kingdom
Where basil and heliotrope burst into bloom,
Where gardens and orchards and arbors and bowers
Are bordered by hedgerows besprinkled with flowers,
Beyond golden wheatfields arise shining towers
Which beckon the roadweary soldier or pilgrim
To rest in the peace of this bountiful kingdom
The kitchens of which roast fat chickens and sheep,
Great fires warm the chambers where grandmothers
        sleep,
Sweet music and merriment sing through this king-
        dom,
Where a stout little dwarf will creep out of a pie.
And war does not visit this peaceable kingdom,
Its gates are warped open, the portcullis high.

(trio): High up   High rise
         And high over   The towers
         This peaceable kingdom   O'er bowers
         Shine the bluest   Of flowers
         And brightest   Which glimmer
         Of skies.   Like gems
                                        At the sky.

                    Hie thee
                    Back home
                    With thy burgeoning baskets
                    Of green beans
                    And barley
                    And rye.

Basil and   Foolery,
Heliotrope,   Drollery,
Ripe plums   Dwarves on
And berries,   White ponies
Perfume the air   Lead the
Of this   Parades of the
Peaceable kingdom.   Peaceable kingdom.

                    Normans and
                    Saracens
                    Are subject
                    Of song,
                    But do not
                    Bear arms to the
                    Peaceable kingdom.

Chorus: A son has been given the lord of the manor,
         A beautiful boy and an heir to his bounty,
         At the babe's first cry, every finch, thrush, and swallow,
         Each goose and each swan, each bright bird in the hollow

19

Took at once to the skies o'er the breadth of the county.
Towers and battlements and paving stones rang
As above a shrill greeting, or warning, they sang.
Some said there was fear in it, others said joy,
A miraculous calling for the sire's new boy,
Who would grow in his promise, increase in his skill,
In his scholarship, piety—adept at the kill.
Such an easy young horseman, pride of the kingdom,
His bow slung behind him, a hawk on his wrist,
How he flew to the forests, this boy spirit, Julian.

(trio):   A son, a seed;   Swallows swoop
             A seed, a son;   And rabbits run,
             Blessings, sire,   Awake to
             From the   The cries
             Blessed One.   Of Julian.

The priest
In his vigil,
The prayerful nun,
Hark to the
Warning the
Birds have sung.

A fearful   From the doe
Joy is   A cry,
Raised this day.   From her buck
Hear all the   A bray,
Animals,   Julian
Hear them pray.   Is born today.

A seed, a son,
A saint
We pray,
Julian takes
The hunter's
Way.

Chorus: Comes Julian cantering into the wood,
Covered by nightfall and earth and blood.
Not one handful of years past the baptismal fount
Before the young esquire saddled his mount,
And was master of spaniel, retriever, and dane.
Frothing, eyes rolling, they race the demesne
After hare, boar, and stag, now ripped, now broken,
Strewn by the wayside, complaints unspoken,
As silently broadsword lifts up the heads
From downy breasts of owls asleep,
Or cuts the legs sharply from under the cranes,
Or hacks away tufted tails for tokens,
While the lord and his lady are dreaming asleep.

(trio): Deep in   Sleep
The night   If thou darest,
And deep in   Panther, serpent,
The forest,   Death
Arises a terror   Or oblivion,
Which has no voice.   That is thy choice.

Keep
Thy vigil
For master
Julian;
For a hunter
So true
Must God rejoice.

Horse and hounds   Wolf and weasel.
Thunder   Badger
The thickets,   And beaver,
Pheasant   Fox
And partridge   And ferret
Ascend   Fly
Like prayers.   From their lairs.

Lord and lady,
Monk
And abbot,
Cotter
And sheriff
Sleep
Unawares.

(Tenor alone. Julian *enters.)*

(tenor): Behold, Julian!
Son and heir,
The treasure of my sire.
No prince was made more fair,
No hunter made more daring,
A penitant unsparing,
A heart of pure desire.

Julian: Yes, Julian, behold:
"The treasure of my sire."
Would his treasure were pure as gold,
Would that I could name my dark desire . . .

And yes, by night I hunt,
Moved, methinks, by what moves storms.
It is, I know, my raised arm,
My blade upon the tender throat,
My spur upon my mount's warm flank.
I, Julian.

But what moves Julian?
Am I some demon's raised arm? His blade?
Spurred as surely as I spur—nay, deeper,
For as yet no steed hath set a pace to please me,
None yet so swift as wind,
Though wild at night I would surpass the wind.

Is it I, gentle Julian,
Who tendered cooing pigeons in their cages?
Whose fair hand neatly copied out his lessons?
Who in devotion cannot staunch his tears?
Whose courtesy and quiet are his lady mother's
        pleasure?
Whose quick delight in arms his sire's "treasure"?

I, Julian.
Pray, but hear the truth about this prayerful page.

(*A chapel altar and communion rail. A small boy,
dressed in Julian's colors, reenacts the story of the slay-
ing of the white mouse.*)

At mass one morning in my seventh year,
I spied a mouse beneath the altar rail.
Pure white it was, intent
Upon the fallen crumbs of blessed bread.
Each sabbath morning faithfully it came,
And on the third, when prayer was done, I struck it
        dead.

It took no heavy blow to free its soul.
The blood spilt on its pelt was ruby red.
That single droplet crimsoned all the world,
And out beyond the oaken chapel doors
The creatured world, on wing and hoof and claw,
Called Julian! As if unto a war.

In every kill a vaulting, dreadful joy,
The strangled heron thrills within my grasp,
Beneath the velvet of their broken skulls,
Panthers speak their final mortal yes.
And wilder, never weary of the sport,
I dream of greater kills the while I rest.

(*Enter male chorus with Julian's* father.)

Chorus: Sire, young Julian has come of an age
           When the arts of the hunt are acquired.
           His wit rises quickly to trackings and markings,
           His kit is as fine as the noblest squire's,

           With thy kennel of Breton dogs, greyhounds, and
                      boarhounds,
           Mastiffs from Tartary, spaniels and beagles;
           With Caucasion hawks, Babylonian sakers,
           And gerfalcons truer than arrows, than eagles!

(quartet):   Fetch   Set
              The bag-nets,   The pointers,
              Baits and traps,   Spread
              Hone   The netting,
              The hardwood   Rouse
              For our snares!   The quail,
                                       Bag the hares!

              Beat   Let pipes
              The drum   And horns
              Before   And blood-
              The foxes,   Fed voices
              Clamp   Shatter
              The claws   Frozen
              Of lynx   Morning air!
              And bears!

Father: But sirs, do ye not see?
           The boy declines to hunt with thee.
           Young Julian would ride alone,
           His bow behind, his belted blade,
           His snow-white Scythian falcon
           Tethered tightly to his lesser hand.

Not for meat does Julian slaughter,
Nor to move his goodly frame,
Nor to rid the wilds of danger,
But slays as might a holy martyr
Offering prayer as he is slain.

(Father *and his party exeunt. In the shadows below
four stags in antlers are seen in an enclosure of rock.*)

Julian: No, not for meat or sport or pleasure
Am I driven to the kill.
No, astride, full gallop,
I am of another will,
Yes! Another will burns in my breast,
Another strength draws back the bowstring,
Guides this dagger twixt the ribs
Of lions in their rage.

Yet it is I who feels the joy—
Yes, joy!
A joy surpassing words,
As when this wintry dawn
I flew before the freezing wind
And, sword aloft,
Cut rooks dead in their frozen sleep.

Dismounting at a precipice,
I drew my dagger from by belt
And fell upon a pair of goats.
The first lept deathward;
His trembling mate received my steel
In the sorrow of her heart.

There below I saw a sight:
(*Stags move, grow restless*)
A dozen, a score, no a hundred stags,

Enclosed three ways by rock as sheer as ice.
Into this canyon's mouth I crept,
Then rose to standing height.

(*A figure, dressed in* Julian*'s colors, approaches the
stags, driving them back.*)

Their cries were as a man on fire,
As through a forest of their flanks,
Their rearing haunches, lowered racks,
I carved my crimson way.

(*Yet another stag, bigger than the others, appears.*)

And when the last had shivered forth his soul,
I turned to behold one greater still.
An arrow pierced his lifeless fawn,
His doe's warm blood steamed round my feet.

(*The* Julian *figure pierces the stag's head with his final
arrow. The stag bellows. The sound is as piercing and
rich as a horn.*)

Enraged, my final arrow buried in his brow,
The great soul sprang—
And stopped still.

Eyes aflame, it spoke as though a man,
Thrice it cursed me:
(A bell tolls)

Stag: Accursed! Accursed! Accursed!
Some day, ferocious soul,
Thou wilt murder thy father and thy mother.

(*The stag drops to its forelegs and expires. A shaft of
light illuminates only* Julian.)

26

Julian: No, no, no, no!
           By my will, by Christ,
           This crime will not be so.

           Still, supposing that was my desire?

           (*From the castle battlements, Julian's* mother *and fa-
           ther peer out, looking for their son.* Julian *drops to his
           knees, as the bell tolls in the mounting darkness.*

           Daylight. Father *and* Mother *are holding court before
           full chorus. In soft light* Julian *lies abed in his
           chamber.*)

Chorus: The master's sorry soul is sick,
           He lies abed unmoving, mute.
           He refuseth honey, meat, and fruit
           And turneth not to fool or lute.

Father, :   Seek not the cause,
Mother   Nor, pray, complain of this,
           But answer with our prayerful faith
           That Julian will join with Christ in saving
                   health.

Chorus: Christ's will be done, and soon we pray,
           For some vile venom works in him
           That such a youth should lie the day,
           As though his soul hath flown away.

Mother: No more of poison, pray, my friends.
           Best we not divert him?

Father: If he be Julian, a tempered blade
           Will light the melancholic eye.

(Descends stairs, removes a Saracen saber, hanging decoratively over the arched portal leading to Julian's chamber.

As chorus sings, Julian's father reaches his son's bedside where he presents the saber. Julian's gaze fixes on the blade. Slowly, he sits up, one hand on his father's shoulder, the other on the saber. The father exits.)

Chorus: A blade to light the dreamer's eye,
A blade to wake the weary wight,
Bright token of the art of arms,
A beacon through thy dreary night.

Awake to arms, dear Julian,
Arise to manly sport once more,
Take up thy sword, bold Julian,
Again to the hare, the bear, the boar!

Again thy mount, again thy horn,
In arms thy will is done.
For thus was noble Julian born,
For arms and arms alone.

Julian: *(Holding saber, rises)*
No! I shall not!
Have I no other strength than this?
This is a blade.
This blade is steel.
It is not I.

But in its absence—what?
I, Julian.
Alive to the chase,
Alive to the kill,
But dead to gentle duty

And cursed to—
No! I shall not!

(*He wheels and slashes the saber mightily, the gesture turning him about. The stroke narrowly misses his father who stops short beneath the archway. Julian drops in a faint. Darkness.*

Chorus has congregated in the courtyard, while up on the battlements, Julian *looks out over the ramparts.*)

Chorus: One month ill lay Julian, dying,
(female   A soul grows cold,
  voice)   a fire dies.

(second: Two months ill young Julian, lying,
 female   Ash and ember
 voice)   In his eyes.

  (all):   A soul grows cold,
                A fire dies,
                Ash and ember
                In his eyes.
                O hear his lady mother's cries:
                In his eyes
                May ash be ember.

(female: Three months ill lay Julian, healing,
  voice)   Ember glowing,
                Flame be praised.

(second: His lady mother's prayerful will
 female   Didst Julian,
 voice)   Like Lazarus, raise.

29

(all):   Ash to ember,
             Coal to flame,
             Blessed be our Lady's name.

*(The wings of a white stork appear to flutter and come
to rest on the top of an inner courtyard wall. Julian
seizes a javelin and hurls it at the bird. It impales his
mother's high peaked cap, nailing it to the oaken
woodwork. Chorus shrieks in horror. A bell begins to
toll.)*

(female: It is my lady's head dress!
 voice)   And in a swoon she lies.
             What demon's work in this?

*(Julian bolts down the battlement steps and flees. The
bell tolls more loudly.)*

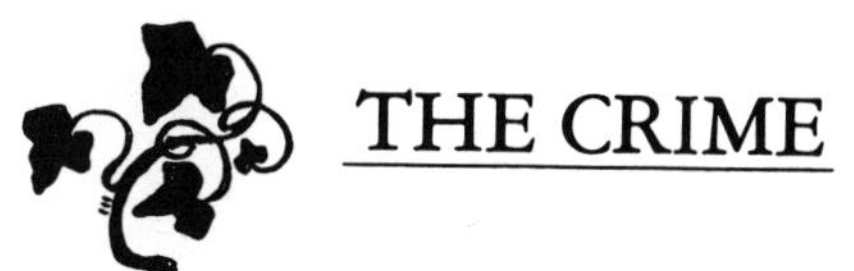

THE CRIME

(The wide world. The red cross of the Crusaders flies from the battlements of a fortress abroad. Below, the terrain is stark and wild.)

Chorus: The world is a wonder,
The wonder is war,
To arms, for God, to arms!
Across oceans and deserts
Bearing thunder
In arms, sweet Christ, in arms!

The infidel bears a thousand heads,
The infidel wears a thousand faces,
The infidel stains the horizon red,
The infidel lives in a thousand places.

Infidel! Infinite infidel
Beckons us.
Infidel, terrible summons
We hearest.
For our Lord Savior,
Gentlest, Dearest,
We fly to thy throat,
To thy gut, to thy loin,
Like birds to thy battlements,
Fish to thy moats,
Offer our blood
In thy crucified name.

O infidel, infinite infidel,
Behold!

(Julian appears, sword raised)

A warrior charmed,
A prince of the kill.
Never hast arrow flown more true,

Nor dagger pierced more deadly through
The helm or the heart of an infidel.
His might conjoined with holy will,
O holy will, sacred kill,
Behold, lord Julian—rampant!

Julian: My fellows and my friends,
           Have we not heard din of battles?
           Trodden over dying men?
           Set foot and sail for harder glories
           Not yet by any Christian seen?

Chorus: Behold! Behold the man
           Who sleweth Oberbirbach's dragon
           And the serpent of Milan.

Julian: I bid thee battle forth in Christ,
           I bid thee take no blameless life,
           No child, no clerk in prayer,
           No gentle sire, nor wife—
           No! None of these, but forth
           With me to break and banish
           Christ-less souls from all the earth!

Chorus: We march behind the man
           Who sleweth Oberbirbach's dragon
           And the serpent of Milan.

           (*The* Emperor *and his* daughter *appear, in flight, on
           the ramparts above. They are taken by four armed
           Saracens.*)

Julian: Aloft and to it then!

Chorus: Woe unto the Saracen!

*(They battle hand-to-hand on the upper battlements
until the Saracens and one of Julian's followers lie
slain. Julian steadies his furious comrades.)*

Julian: Cease now,
For these be silent.
I can feel their souls
Arising round like prayers,
And this fair soul

(Kneels by his slain comrade)

Is beamed like radiant arrow
To the Sacred Heart of hearts.
How strange, how blessed is this dying,
An offering so like—prayer.
To think: one's soul in air.

Chorus: Thus thy soldier gives to thee:
In prayerful slaughter
Souls set free,

And when we give up mortal breath,
Like these, we rise
From prayerful death.

(Emperor, his daughter enter)

(solo voice):   Sire, look there.
Pray, put aside thy grief.
Comes the emperor
To speak of his relief.

Julian: *(Kneels before Emperor)*
My lord, God bless thee.
We are a party of knights in Christ
At war upon the infidel.
Thy peace we would restore,

Thy kingdom's sweet solemnity.
I am Julian,
By my Savior's grace
A vassal of the blessed Christ.

Emperor: Arise, Julian.
In courage as in courtesy
Thou glorifies thy holy Liege.
Thou breakest an accursed siege.
By God's grace in thee
Have I lived to see this day—
And this beloved child free.

(Daughter *steps forward*)

Julian: My lady,
We ask thou might forgive
Our deadly, noisesome coming.
Not in vengeful anger
But to cut the faithless cancre
From thy rightful realm
Didst we trespass here.

Now quiet and restored,
May thou grant us leave
And thus commence again thy civil peace
And Christian harmony.

Daughter: Courteous Julian,
Thy will be done
With our Godspeed.
But pray, wilt thou not rest awhile?
Take shelter here from storm and battle,
Salve thy wounds in sun and sea,
Sup on thy deserved bounty,
Receive our hospitality?

Emperor: The child bespeaks her father's heart.
            Wouldst thou, Julian, stay?
            Wouldst thou were my very son.
            Wilt thou, soldier, pray?

Julian, :   O war is a wonder,
Daughter   The wonder is why
            A youth is spared,
            While others die.

                    O youth be spared
                    Let others perish,
                    Pray leave them where they lie.

            A youth is a wanderer
            Cursed to kill
            As purely as would
            His Savior's will.

                    We curse thee not,
                    O ease thy heart,
                    Beloved heart be still.

            A curse is to wander,
            Yet wandering here
            I come to a rest
            I crave, yet fear.

                    Fear not thy sweet, deserved rest.
                    Lay down thy arms,
                    Thy brow to my breast.

            Aye! I will!
            I will have this trophy, peace.
            I shall stalk serenity
            With a tiger's eye.

Comrades, go with God.
And may Christ Jesus grant me sweet release
And thee a new Jerusalem,
And ever after peace.

Chorus: Bless thee, sire.
And likewise go with God,
Who alone in majesty doth know thy heart.
We go now to our destined peril,
We warriors depart.

(*Exeunt.* Julian *looks after them. He holds his sword
out before him with both hands, then drops it.*

*The court of the Emperor's Mediterranean kingdom.
There are benches, tapestries, greenery, and every-
where bowls of brilliant fruit. In contrast to the house-
hold of Julian's youth, this opulence is Mediterranean:
brighter, paler, more languid.*)

Chorus: This is the kingdom of rest and reason,
This is the realm where time goes on,
Where the babe becometh youth,
Where the youth becometh man,
Where the sea grinds pebbles to powdery dunes,
Where winds wash red to pale rose,
Where lizards sun, where cats repose.
This is the land of soft sea winds,
Pungent with spices from Africa.

These are the sands where the sea begins,
This is the shore where sorrow ceases,
This is the light that whitens the world,
This is a place to wait, to listen,
This is a place to still thy heart.

Chorus: Fine as sand,   Tender
 (trio)   Soft as blossom,   As thy lady's
           Still   Hand
           Thy troubled heart.   Upon thy burning
                                      brow.

                       Castle, cloister
                       Tinted rose
                       By sunset's
                       Gentle art.

Rest where seas
Glide blue   On alabaster
And curling   Colonnade
In from   Lean thy
The yawning deep.   Fevered cheek.

                       Tide and Zephyr,
                       Rising,
                       Falling,
                       Good Julian
                       Asleep.

                     (*Emperor's* daughter *appears*)

(all):   Here is the salve to every burning,
        Here is the pool to bathe thy heat,
        Here is the thousandfold returning,
        Here the reward for youth's chaste journey,
        The gentlest caress borne on silent feet.
        More silent and softer than cloud she envelops thee,
        A vastness of verdure reclines lush before thee,
        Draws thee forth into an infinite sweetness
        Where vaulting release of a weakness most welcome
        Gentles and tenders thy wound-weary form.
        From lavender dusk to the gold shaft of dawn
        Entering, entering, pleasure on pleasure,

Entering wholly the ease of the Other,
Sweet union of which thou wast born.

(trio): Beckoning,   Entering,
         Beckoning   Entering
         Pleasure   Waters
         On Pleasure,   Of ecstasy,
         Julian, surrender. Julian,
                             Unfasten thy cloak.

                  Falling
                  And falling
                  Through endless
                  Oblivion,
                  Julian,
                  Repose.

         Release,   Cease,
         Release   Cease
         Thy rage   Thy hurtful
         And thy righteousness, Hardness,
         Thy calm   Enter
         Shall be complete. Easeful sleep.

                  Peace,
                  Peace
                  Lay thy brow
                  To my breast.
                  Weep, warrior,
                  Weep.

(all):   Here is a home, a pilgrim's haven,
         Here is a scented, earthly heaven,
         Here lies the land of blossom, not blade,
         Here grows the plum, the orange, the melon,
         Warm in this sunlight, repose in this shade.
         Here stands a maid with the visage of Helen,

Here flourish the comforts that hands have made.
Make this thy rest, thy peace, thy dwelling,
Rule here with justice, beloved by the ruled,
Hold court in majesty, gilded and jeweled,
By fair afternoon walk thy verdant estates,
Open to pilgrims thy generous gates,
Hear the pure voices of penitants swelling.

(trio):   Art on earth,   Enthroned,
          Art in heaven,   Behold
          Rule   Thy fields,
          These pleasant   Thy forests,
          Lands.   Thine opulent
                                  Expanse.

                            Incline thine eye
                            In gratitude
                            For all
                            Thy Savior
                            Grants.

Rest and reason   Plum and berry,
Rule thy heart,   Orange and melon,
School thy   Full
Troubled soul   And ripe
In peace.   And sweet.

                            Rule in justice,
                            Rest in comfort
                            All is
                            Order,
                            All is ease.

                            (*Chorus exuent.* Julian *enters.*)

Julian: Thus now am I blessed,
          With this gentle ease, this rest,

These towers, these lands,
Their ripe delicious fruits.

And this is peace.
For my company and my comfort,
A lady wife, who is kindness in flesh,
Airy soft as one born
Of this land's light
And sea breeze mild.
The day long and the night
Smiling, tending, asking not
But that I am pleased.
In her full sweetness I repose
As I might immersed in scented waters.

My troth is thus an easeful rest,
As if at pleasure's very core
Was a stillness,
Was a death.

(The bell tolls faintly. Julian starts, as if he hears something in the bush before him. He moves stealthily toward it, feeling for his absent dagger. His attention is suddenly diverted by something flying overhead. Again, reflexively, he reaches over his shoulder for an arrow from his imaginary quiver.)

Yet—still—my eye is sharp
For the leopard's lemon eye,
No eagle draws its arc across the sky
That I do not, like remembered arrow,
Pierce its cagèd heart.

O! There is no peace in this.
Nor, by Christ, can I do harm
Bearing no forged or crafted weapon,
Following no call to arms.

Wife: What troubleth thee, my lord?
         The day be bright, but thou art dark.
         Let me know thy will
         That I may ease the lack.

Julian: Good woman, lady wife,
         Thy Julian lacks for nought,
         And as for Ease,
         She greets him smiling all about

         And bids him rest
         And doth his every gesture bless;
         All here is gentle, temperate—
         Lest Ease herself be excess.

Wife: Good husband, this doleful talk
         Dost turn darkly on itself,
         Sweet ease and quiet
         Can indeed be excess
         As honey overthickened
         Or melons sickly overripe.
         Lest ease be torpor
         Awake, good soldier!
         Arouse thy fabled appetite.
         By thy sword our ancient foes
         Have all been purged or pacified.
         Thy peace will reign a thousand years,
         Yet there be inland forests dark,
         And swift across enchanted fens
         Awaits a world of prey
         To chase in glorious sport.
         Go, direct thy warrior's will
         To this ancient manly art.

Julian: Good wife, I must decline
         Thy loving remedy.

In hunting lies my soul's very doom.
In that terrible, taunting play
Am I consumed.
Nay, I cannot!

Wife: Doomed in hunting?
          My lord undone by tusk or claw?

Julian: More deeply doomed.
          For it has been foretold
          That I would shed the mortal blood
          Of those who gave me life.

Wife: This, my husband, cannot be,
          For this I truly know of thee:
          However swift and cruel thine arm,
          Thy generous heart seeks no man's harm.

Julian: No harm, no bloodshed
          Do I will,
          But in arms I am moved
          By a mystery.
          I tire not,
          And, unfeeling, kill
          As if weightless in a sleeping dream.
          O, in mere remembering
          I come awake.

Wife: Awake? I see thou art.
          My husband, do thy studied will.   (*She exits.*)

(*There is the bark and howl of a fox. Julian springs in the direction of the sound, snatching the sword and dagger from their mounting on the wall as he goes. Barks, howls, caws, hisses, and monkey screams mount to an unbearable din.*)

Julian: There, still, the call.
           Hear them, their flickering souls
           Who call me thus.
           I know their calls,
           Though these wilds be strange.
           O hear them!
           Each voice a beckoning flame!
           Into the night then—
           Nor shall I return
           Before each candle's out!   (*He exits.*)

(In the darkness, a pounding on oaken doors grows increasingly insistent. Light comes up very faintly on a bedchamber, where Julian's wife has retired for the night. She sits up, alarmed, then rises.)

Wife: Good Julian, is it thee?
           He wouldst not thus announce
           His rightful coming.
           Who comes then?
           Enter! And speak thy urgency.

(The arched door opens. A servant carrying a torch leads in an elderly man and woman, Julian's mother and father.)

Servant: My lady,
           Forgive this late disturbance.
           For news at night,
           However sweet,
           Is too often fearsome
           In our startled hearts.

           I trespass thus
           That these two may give voice
           To urgent errand.

Wife: Thou trespass not,
For I am full awake.
My husband's absence
Lighteneth my sleep.

I bid thee welcome, pilgrims.
Though thou arrivest late,
My man shall see to thy refreshment.
Then dwell with us a while.
Most find this kingdom fair.
Then, when thou hath rested well,
Let us have thy news.

Father: By thy leave, good lady,
We beg of thee a word.
I know the hour is late,
As is, we fear, the hour of our lives,
For we are dim of eye
And thin of bone.
Our steps on this world's path
Now leave a brief impression.

Wife: And yet thy gentle bearing
Speaks thee well.

Father: Gentle bearing comes from gentle born.
Good lady, hear me on.
In northern kingdom fair and ample
Didst we dwell,
A lord and lady
Long ere we were pilgrims.
A son and heir we bred
Until he grew to fearsome potency.

Mother: Devout he was and fair
Of form and face,

No youth or knight
Could match him in the chase.

But darkness did torment
His gracious heart.
He wouldst swoon and lie abed
The day and night,

Father: Until at gruesome accident
He fled,
And vowed for all his life
To dwell apart.

In God's service
And by His knowing grace
Didst Julian, our son, win fame in arms.

Mother: Stories of his deeds
Have led us hither,
Long years afoot
Through every wearing clime.

Father: O, is it so?
Doth Julian dwelleth here?
Hath providence
Granted our journey's end?

Mother: To touch his cheek,
To clasp once more his hand.
It is this and only this
We ask of him.

Father: That he be here,
Beloved Julian,
Didst we pilgrims bear
Our prayerful way to thee.

Wife: O, this be much to hear.
          Of his dame and sire in the north
          My troubled husband
          Speaketh not.

          Yet worn and pallid,
          Thinly shrouded,
          And barefoot as thou art,
          Do I not see Julian's fire
          Glowing in thine asking eyes?

          His excellence
          In chase and arms
          Thou vividly recallest.
          And his name—Julian.
          I see no snare or wile in this.
          Thou wantest not,
          Thou layest not a claim.

          O yes, yes!
          In my very heart of hearts
          I sense ye be
          Lord Julian's sire and dame!   (*They embrace.*)

Father, : Praise God! This tearful journey blessed,
 Mother   Our Julian, estranged and found,
           Dost grant us gentle rest.

   Wife: Gentle rest I bid thee take
           Upon this very honored couch,
           That on the morn
           When ye awake
           Ye wake to Julian's embrace.

Father, : Doth he in some near chamber sleep?
 Mother   O to cast an aged eye
           Upon his visage in repose.

Wife: Alas, he does not lie abed this night,
For at my urging he has gone to hunt.
Soon he shall return, his melancholy shed,
To embrace his very blood in morning light.

Sleep well, good lord and lady,
And when at last ye wakest,
Arise to blessèd joy!

(Wife *exits. Father and* mother *recline on the offered bed, drawing a coverlet over themselves as lights dim on the sleeping chamber.*

A cacaphony of animal voices is heard again, growing steadily louder. A Chorus of animals—big cats, deer, weasels and serpents—precede Julian *onto the stage. The entourage of animals huddle close to him as he walks, a serpent slithering about his feet.*)

Julian: What is the will of this bestial enchantment?
Who presseth these brutes to me?
Sloweth my way?
Why do they not make an end of me,
Meal of me? Celebrate
Vengefully huntsman as prey?

(trios):   No cat in the jungle,
No swamp-regal serpent,
No wolf of the steppe,

        No razor-beaked eagle,
        No venom-toothed viper,
        No boar in his rutting

(all):   Dost muse on thy slaughter,
Wouldst hurt for the hurting.

Julian, Julian,
'Tis thee who wouldst kill
For the merciless ecstasy,

Thee who would pierceth
The heart of creation,
Thee who would pierceth
The eye of the sun.

Julian, :   My holy Lord and Savior,
Chorus   Thy will be done and not my own.

Julian, Julian,
It is thee!

If the taunts of brutes
Be purgative,
Cleanse me thus.
My very life I offer up
If that wouldst by thy will.

Was it, by some mystery, for Thee
I hunted so?
For Thee I battled tireless
Under crimson cross?

Julian, Julian,
It is thee!

Aye, sin to say,
I felt it was,
As though, like perfect penitant,
I could kill the living cleft between
Thy holy Self and mine.

Julian, Julian,
It is thee!

Yet this cursèd night
Thou tells me no.
For in forest dark this night
My sword and dagger break
Upon the very fur of lynx and bear,
My arrows wobble weakly in the air,
My javelin snaps dryly as a stick.

> Julian, Julian,
> It is thee!

How close they follow now,
Like all their kindred souls returned.
> (*Chorus's chanting ceases.*)

Chorus: How thou killed us,
    Julian, Julian!
    Killing us, Julian,
    Again and again,
    Sensing the spark
    That each killing kindles,
    A mote of the brilliance
    Of infinite Afterwards.

    In each kill was a spark,
    Each spark kindled flame,
    Each flame sprouted fire,

    So that heavenward, burning,
    Now mounted, now rampant,
    Thou wouldst render creation
    A purgative pyre.

    Julian, Julian,
    Feel it, feel it,
    The cleansing, purgative fire.

Julian: (*Screams, swings wildly about with his dagger.*)
My God! My God!
Away!   (*Animals flee.*)
Cursèd night.

(*Enters castle, makes his way to his bed chamber, where his* mother *and* father *sleep. Bell begins to toll softly.*)

If this be waking,
Let me be restored in dream.

If there be salve for fever's burning,
If there be comfort deep,
It is my gentle, healing lady,
Who lies in untormented sleep.

(*Kneeling, he caresses what he thinks to be his wife's cheek, but feels instead his father's beard. In a strangled whisper:*)

What's this?
Hoary beard where silken cheek should lie?
Another in my place!
O yes! And did she not,
Urging my relief,
Bid me off to hunt this cursèd night.
This cursèd night!

Chorus: Entering, entering
Waters of ecstasy . . .

Beckoning, beckoning
Pleasure on pleasure . . .

Release, release
Thy rage and thy righteousness,
Thy calm shall be complete.

Julian: Cursèd night!   (*Unsheathing his dagger*)
Benighted curse!
Taunt me no more!
An end to thee!

(*Enraged,* Julian *stabs the sleeping figures repeatedly.
As he does so, his* wife *enters, aghast.*)

Wife: Julian! Julian!
Cease! Cease!

(Julian *rises, uncomprehending. He looks from his
wife to the figures in the bed. He tears back the coverlet and beholds his murdered parents. Bell stops.*)

Julian: Thy will be done!

(*Drops dagger, makes the sign of the cross. Turns to
his wife, fallen to her knees in grief and disbelief.*)

Woman, do not approach me,
Nor answer my words,
Nor cast thine eyes upon my face or form.
Tend gently
To the sacramental rites
Of these two slain—
Though this very dawn
They wake in heaven.   (*Exits.*)

(*Chorus place* Julian's father *and* mother *on burial lit-
ters, shrouding them, and carry them to an altar that
has been arranged up on the battlements.*)

Chorus: A son and heir
(trio)   They bred,
           He grew
           To fearsome
           Bearing.

Devout he was
And fair,
No youth
Or knight
His match.

But darkness
Did torment him.
He vowed
To dwell
His life apart.

Their steps
Upon their
Pilgrim's path
Left only
Brief impression.

They callest
At the castle
Late,
The latest hour
Of their lives.

Gentle bearing
Spoke them well,
Gentle
Bearing,
Gentle born.

(all):   Gentle bearing, gentle born,
          Rise like sunshine on the morn.
          Gentle bearing, gentle born,
          Wake in heaven at the dawn.

          (A service is said. As it begins a dark, hooded figure,
          Julian, *enters silently and unnoticed.)*

          I am the resurrection and the life, saith the Lord;
          And he that believeth in me, though he were dead,
              yet shall he live.

And though this body be destroyed, yet I see God;
Whom I shall see for myself and mine eye shall behold
And not as a stranger.

For none of us liveth to himself,
And no man dieth to himself.
For if we live, we live unto the Lord.
And if we die, we die unto the Lord.

Blessed are the dead who die in the Lord;
Even so, saith the Spirit, for they rest from their labors.

(Julian *exits as darkness falls*.)

# THE REPARATION

(*A village market. Chorus, as villeins, are busily and noisily at their crafts and trading benches. It is midday.*)

(first voice):	Idle not, man! (*To his indolent partner*)

(first
voice): Idle not, man!   (*To his indolent partner*)
Quiet fingers
Maketh not
This molten ore
To horse's bit
Or bishop's buckle.
To it, fellow!
To the task.

(second): A prayerful rest
Would not be scorned
By heaven's company.

(*Laughter, taunts from chorus*)

(first): Of heaven's company
Thou wilt little see,
As holy writ makes plain
In Eve and Adam's story.

(all): Ease and plenty,
Rest and pleasure
Are the forfeit
Paid for sin.

Eve and Adam
Lost the garden,
Ease forsaken,
Rest denied.

(trio):   Need and toil,   Carding, spinning,
            Drought and famine,   Blacking, tanning,
            Sowing, reaping,   Weighing, changing,
            Delving, joining   Boiling, baking

                        Frozen winters,
                        Blighted harvest,
                        Blistered children,
                        Bloated swine.

(all):   Hordes of infidels
            Upon us,
            Thunder, plague,
            Our very babes

            A-borning, burning,
            Born to toil,
            Cursèd blessings
            Borne in pain.

third):   Aye, that be our earthly lot
            Until our Savior's foot falls nigh again.

(fourth):   Aye, that is eternity,
            As we reckon hours and days.

(first):   And so I bid thee, idle not!
            But build these stores
            That plague or famine,
            Flame or flood,
            The very darkest curse of men
            Dost not take us
            Early from our mortal plot.

(fifth):   Aye, let us offer
            Grateful prayer

That by God's grace
We dwell this day
In gentle safety.

(all):   O holy Father,
Bless these works
We offer up
To thy approval.

Grant we not,
Like Eve and Adam
Forfeit this,
Our fated toil.

Nor we not,
Like Abel's brother,
Accursed Cain . . .

(*The hooded figure of* Julian *appears. He crosses
himself.*)

(first):   Stay thy dread advance.
Thy garment signals friar poor.
If that be so,
Pray, say thy claim.
Is it bread thou seekest?
A pallet for thy ease?
Thy abbot's alm?

Julian: Good sir,
The meag'rest of these.
For sustaining crust or bitter root
I would bless thee.
Yet I have still a greater need of thee.

Chorus: A greater need, saith he.
         See, we are but villeins at our toil.
         What need couldst it be?

Julian: That ye would hear
         A cursèd man's confession.

(first):   Say it, man.
         Then thou hadst best be gone.

Julian: Hear me.
         I am Julian.
         In another time and kingdom
         Was I gently born.

         In the art of arms
         Didst I excel,
         A virtue born
         Of dark prophetic spell.

         This spell, my curse
         Is like the darkest dream
         Wherein the vilest crime
         Is committed, yet, in sleep, committed not.

         But my dream riseth out of sleep,
         My dream raiseth my right hand,
         My dream plungeth dagger deep
         Unto my very parents' pious hearts!

Chorus: Enough, enough! Be off! Be off! Away, alas, away!

         (*Cowering, they pelt* Julian *with stones and filth.*)

         Like stain,
         Like heavy plague

Cometh he.
Out of hell's foul fissure
Riseth this monstrosity.

(Julian *exits, unhurried*)

Enough! Be off! Away, alas away!

(*Through the darkness, the chorus narrate* Julian's
*journey through the world's desolate places. Through
dreary light, a luminous river emerges. Just above it
stands* Julian's *hovel.*)

Chorus, :
with female
voices

In village and farm and cathedral
    city
Didst Julian speak of his spell and
    his crime.
Shunned and reviled at bridge
    and portal,
Begrudged of a crust, refused at
    the well,
He made his dark way, greeting
    all who would hear him.

Afoot in all weathers, no fire to
    warm him,
No pallet was offered at cottage
    or cloister.
Dogs bared their teeth to him.

Thieves passed him fearfully,

Stones on the path tore the flesh
    from his feet.

Julian,

Perfect pilgrim,

Find me.

Julian, take me

To thy heart.

Julian,

Perfect pilgrim,

Find me.

Julian, take me

To thy heart.

His visage was blistered by mid-
    summer heat,   Julian,
Sinew and flesh fell away from
    his bones,   Perfect pilgrim,
Gaunt now and starvèd, his gar-
    ment worn thin   Find me.
He trod over bramble and boulder
    and marsh   Julian, take me
Through ever more desolate re-
    gions alone.   To thy heart.

In a country more barren than
    fields after fire,   Julian,
More foetid in heat than the
    carnage of battle,   Perfect pilgrim,
So cruelly cold rabbits freeze in
    their warrens,   Find me.
So ravaged by mistrals great oaks
    are upended,   Julian, take me
Here by a river didst Julian retire.   To thy heart.

(Julian *makes his way down the steps to the river bank
where his barge is moored. Merchant travelers hail
him noisily and impatiently.* Julian *poles his barge to
them and ferries them back across.*)

Chorus: Bargeman, hasten! Tend our business.
          Hurry, Bargeman, mind our wares.
          Aid us to our destination,
          Speed us cross this desolation,
          Rid us of the foul damnation
          Hanging in this very air!

          Silent is this mute or mystic.
          Asketh he no toll or fare,
          But toileth on without complaint

In this valley of the shadow
Where mortal souls had best beware.

God go with thee, bargeman.

(*As* Julian *secures his boat to its mooring stake, darkness descends, and he makes his way up the steps to his hovel. The night has grown cold.* Julian *lights a fire. A wintry wind arises, and in its roar* Julian *detects a message.*)

(female
voices):   Julian, perfect pilgrim,
Find me.
Julian take me to thy heart.

Julian, thou hast slain thy father,
Spilt thy tender mother's blood!

(Julian *rises in horror, throws back his hood and cries out. The cry melds into a penetrating cry from below. Illuminated on the far bank, a traveler, the* leper, *is calling to be ferried across the river. Holding a lantern,* Julian *makes his way down to the barge. A storm rages about him as he descends.*)

Leper: Julian!

Julian: I come.

Leper: Julian!

Julian: I come.

Leper: Julian!

Julian: I come.

(*Like the tortured progress of a dream in which motion is inexplicably inhibited,* Julian *and the* leper *make their way across the furious river. As hore at last,* Julian *guides the rag-bound leper out of the barge and up to the hovel.*)

Leper: Julian, I am hungry!

Julian: Take this bread, this broth.

Leper: Julian, I thirst!

Julian: Here is water.
          May it cool thy fevered lips.

Leper: Water, sayest thou?
          Not water this, but wine!
          Drink.

Julian: Wine it hath become.

(Leper *moves to* Julian's *cot, sits*)

Leper: Julian, I am cold!

(Julian *rises, removes his cassock, reducing himself, except for his swaddled groin, to nakedness.*)

Julian: My garment.
          May it warm thee.

Leper: Julian, thy bed!

(Julian *pulls back the counterpane of skins.*)

Julian: Lie here, my father. Rest.

(Leper *lies still for a moment, then throws back the counterpane. Then, with surprising penetration from a man so feeble:*)

Leper: Julian!
Ice runs in my veins.
Lay thyself beside me!

(Julian *gets into the bed. Half-reclining, half-sitting, he caresses the shoulders of the leper to warm him.*)

Julian: As thou wills it, father.
Is there warmth in this?

Leper: Julian, my death is nigh
So cold I grow.
Warm me
With thy body whole!

(Leper *throws his cloak open, revealing his ravaged, suppurating flesh. He lies back, looking skyward, arms extended straight on either side. Julian, pulling back the counterpane, mirrors the leper's position, carefully covering him.*

The instant the bodies of Julian and the leper are joined, head to head, palm to palm, all is dark. Music arises, as a brilliant gothic image brightens overhead, as if in stained glass. It is Julian face to face with the risen Christ. Both figures ascend heavenward in a cruciform shaft of radiant light.)

Chorus: A son is a story,
Each story is true.
In God's great foreknowing
Each story is new.

A son, a seed; a seed, a son;
Blessings, sire, from the blessed One.
Son of thy seed, seed of the Son,
Riseth the good Saint Julian.

In the name of the Father,
The Son,
And the Holy Spirit,
Amen.

Richard A. Hawley studied at Middlebury College, Cambridge University, and Case Western Reserve University, where he completed a Ph.D. in political philosophy. He has published two selections of poems, several books on adolescent development, and various works of fiction, including the novel Headmaster's Papers. St. Julian *will serve as libretto to a musical score by Cleveland composer-conductor Martin Kessler.*

Mary Watson Hawley studied at Middlebury College, The Boston Museum School, and the Cleveland Institute of Art, where she specialized in printmaking. She is currently engaged in book illustration and portraiture. Her work appears frequently in shows and has been acquired by public collections across the country.